PaPerBag
Crafts

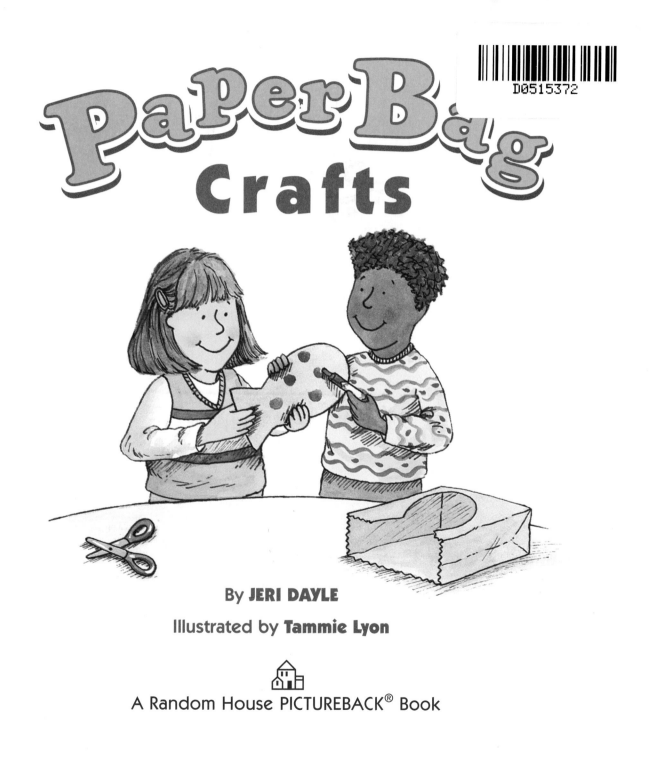

By **JERI DAYLE**

Illustrated by **Tammie Lyon**

A Random House PICTUREBACK® Book

*Dedicated to my daughter Tiffany
and all the children out there
who believe that doing things
that are good for our planet
can also be fun*
—J. D.

*Dedicated to my Mom and Dad,
who always had the time for fun*
—T. L.

Text copyright © 1999 by Jeri Dayle. Illustrations copyright © 1999 by Tammie Lyon.
All rights reserved under International and Pan-American Copyright Conventions.
Published in the United States by Random House, Inc., New York, and simultaneously in Canada by
Random House of Canada Limited, Toronto.

www.randomhouse.com/kids

Library of Congress Cataloging-in-Publication Data
Dayle, Jeri. Paper bag crafts / by Jeri Dayle ; illustrated by Tammie Lyon. p. cm. Summary: Provides
instructions for using paper bags, rubber bands, yarn, and other common materials to make various crafts,
including an aquarium, dinosaur puppet, and bunny.
ISBN 0-679-88644-3 1. Paper work—Juvenile literature. 2. Paper bags—Juvenile literature.
[1. Paper bags. 2. Paper work. 3. Handicraft.] I. Title. TT870.D345 1999 745.54—DC21 98-17180

Printed in the United States of America 10 9 8 7 6 5 4 3 2

PICTUREBACK is a registered trademark of Random House, Inc.

INTRODUCTION

This collection of crafts can easily be made at home by children aged four and up. Some assistance from a parent or teacher when using safety scissors and craft glue will be very helpful. And suggestions from a creative-minded friend of any age are certainly a plus.

Start with a brown paper bag. Add a little imagination. Throw in a few easy extras like rubber bands, yarn, and cotton balls. You'll soon discover a magical mix that yields hours of entertainment!

Marvelous Maracas

You'll be ready to shake, rattle, and roll anytime when you have these marvelous maracas on hand!

What You Need

- 2 cardboard toilet tissue tube rolls

- 2 lunch-size brown paper bags

- non-toxic markers

- 4 rubber bands

- dried peas, beans, or similar filling material

What You Do

1 To make the handles, cut a 3-inch-wide strip from the top of each bag and secure it to one end of each cardboard tube, using a rubber band.

2 Decorate the paper bags by drawing stars, flowers, streamers, or other shapes onto them.

3 Measure about ⅓ cup of the beans (etc.). Pour it into the bag.

4 Insert a cardboard tube into the bag, with the closed end going in first.

5 Close the bag and twist it around the middle of the tube. Then tie it with a rubber band.

6 Repeat steps 3–5 with the second bag and cardboard tube.

7 Ready? Set? Rumba!

Aquarium

Here's a fun way to bring all the color and excitement of a fishtank into your home!

What You Need

- 1 large grocery-size brown paper bag

- Two 8½" x 11" pieces of white paper

- safety scissors

- non-toxic markers

- craft glue

- 1 small piece of green paper or felt

- tape

What You Do

1 Flatten the bag and turn it sideways so the long side is on the bottom. Trace and cut out a large rectangle from the front of the bag, leaving about 2½ inches on all sides. You will have a large framed box that looks like a TV.

2 Using blue and green markers, scribble wavy lines across a sheet of white paper. Then glue it to the inside of the bag so you can see the "water sheet" through the hole in the front.

3 Draw small plants from green paper or felt and cut them out. Then glue them to the front of the bag at the bottom corners of the hole.

4 To fill your aquarium, draw little fish (1 to 2 inches long) on the other sheet of white paper. Color them in and cut them out.

5 Loop a small piece of tape behind your fish and tape them directly on the water.

6 If you like, add a little treasure chest made from felt and sequins.

Dinosaur Puppet

Here's an easy way to make a friend you'll treasure for eons.

What You Need

- 1 lunch-size brown paper bag
- 1 small piece of red paper
- safety scissors
- non-toxic markers
- tape or craft glue
- one 8½" x 11" sheet of yellow or green paper

What You Do

1 Put your hand inside the bag so the crease in the bag is between your thumb and fingers.

2 To make the dinosaur's tongue, cut a 2-inch-long oval from the sheet of red paper. Glue one end of the oval to the crease so that it sticks out.

3 To make the dinosaur spikes, cut out six 1-inch triangles from the yellow or green paper.

4 Now flatten out the bag. Take one triangle and glue it to the top of the bag. Then glue the rest of the triangles, about ½ inch apart, down the dinosaur's back.

5 Use your markers to draw two big eyes on the bottom flap. You can also add scales and any other dino features you like.

Wrap It Up

What could be more special than
this easy wrapping paper you make yourself?

What You Need

- 1 large grocery-size brown bag
- safety scissors
- 2 old sponges (dry)
- "childproof" paint in at least 3 colors
- bowls for the paint

What You Do

1 Remove the bottom flap of the paper bag.

2 Cut the bag open along a side seam.

3 Cut heart, star, flower, diamond, and circle shapes from the old sponges.

4 Dip the sponges into the bowls of paint, then blot onto the paper.

5 When the paint patterns are dry, wrap a gift in this one-of-a-kind wrapping paper that you made all by yourself!

Night Owl Windsock

Have a hoot putting together
this little night-owl friend!

What You Need

- 1 large grocery-size brown paper bag
- safety scissors
- 1 old cardboard egg carton
- 1 small piece of yellow paper
- craft glue
- non-toxic markers
- string
- masking tape

What You Do

1 Cut a large rectangle out of the bottom of the bag, about ½ inch in from all sides.

2 Cut out two sections from the egg carton to use for the owl's eyes. Color the centers a nice, glowing green.

3 Next, glue the egg-carton eyes near the new "top" of your bag.

4 To make the beak, cut a 2-inch triangle from the yellow paper. Bend two of the corners back and tape or glue them to your bag, just under the eyes.

5 To make strips that blow in the breeze, cut slits about 7 inches long and ½ inch apart all along the "bottom" of the bag.

6 To complete the owl, draw little feather-like "V"s using the brown and orange markers.

7 To hang up your night owl, tape two 11-inch strings inside the head on the shorter sides of the rectangles, and two 8-inch strings on the longer sides.

8 Then tie all four strings together, about 2 inches from the top, forming a small loop. Use the loop to hang your windsock up where it can catch the breeze.

Goldfish Piñata

This colorful fish-shaped
piñata will make you the "hit" of the party!

What You Need

- 1 large grocery-size brown paper bag

- 1 small piece of red felt

- safety scissors

- 2 large pompoms

- 1 small roll of crepe paper, in a good fish color (yellow, orange, or silver)

- tape

- candies or small toys

- 1 "scrunchie" band

What You Do

1 Open up the bag and lay it on the table sideways. Then flatten it out.

2 To make the fish's mouth, cut two small "B" shapes from your red felt. Glue them on the bottom of either side of the crease with the rounded side facing out.

3 To make the fish's eyes, glue one large pompom on either side of the bag.

4 To put the scales on your fish, use crepe paper. Tape one end of the crepe paper to the top of the bag. Then twist the crepe paper to get a scaly effect and wrap it around the bag. Tape the other end of the crepe paper down.

5 Repeat step 4 with the rest of the strips of crepe paper, until there are 3 inches left at the open end of the bag.

6 Fill the bag with candies or small toys and close the bag with a large scrunchie band. Tie a string around your piñata and hang it from a tree limb. Swat at the piñata with a broom handle. When it bursts open, grab the treats and enjoy!

Bags Bunny

Storing your toys, jewelry, and goodies is neat <u>and</u> fun when you make this little bunny sack.

What You Need

- 1 lunch-size brown paper bag

- safety scissors

- non-toxic markers or crayons

- 1 large cotton ball or pompom

- 1 small pompom

What You Do

1 From the top of the bag, cut 4 inches down along the crease at each corner.

2 From this new edge, cut straight around to the back of the bag. Do not cut the back.

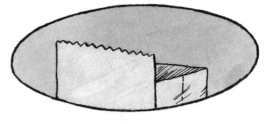

3 To make the ears, cut a "V" down the middle of the front of the bag. The bottom of the "V" should be on the same level as the top of the new back of the bag. You will have a cone-shaped piece left. Save it.

4 Using your markers or crayons, color the insides of the ears and draw on eyes and whiskers.

5 Glue on a small pompom for a nose. For the bunny's tail, turn the bag around and glue the large pompom (or cotton ball) to the middle of the back.

6 To make the bunny's feet, take the cone shape you saved and cut it in half. Glue one foot to each side of the front flap, with the straight edge on the bottom.

Tortoise Footstool

What's green, fluffy, and great for resting?
A tortoise footstool!

What You Need

- 1 large grocery-size brown paper bag
- safety scissors
- non-toxic markers or stickers
- stapler
- 2 full bags of cotton balls, pillow filling, or other stuffing material

What You Do

1 To begin, flatten the bag, including its flap, out on a table, then cut off the corners at the top of the bag and at the bottom.

2   Take the corners you cut and cut them in half along the hinge. You will have eight triangles.

3   To make the tortoise's head, use one triangle. Staple it to the end of the bag with the flap on it.

4   To make the tortoise's feet, use four more triangles. Insert the first one into the seam of the bag about one-third of the way down on the right side. Staple it in place, closing off the seam.

5   Repeat step 4 farther down on the right side. Then take two more triangles and repeat on the left side.

6   Staple all around three sides of the bag, leaving the end open. Fill your tortoise with stuffing material so it's nice and fat and the shell puffs up on top.

7   Use one more triangle for the tail. Insert it into the middle of the open part and staple it. Then staple the opening shut.

8   Decorate your tortoise with markers or stickers, drawing in toenails, eyes, and so on. Don't forget to make a nice pattern on the back of his shell!

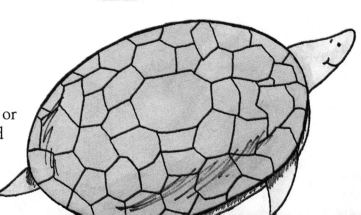

Truly Paper Doll

This paper bag friend will make a stunning addition to your doll collection!

What You Need

- 1 lunch-size brown paper bag
- safety scissors
- non-toxic markers or stickers
- about 1 yard (36") of string or yarn
- craft glue or glue stick
- 1 scrap of lace or fabric

What You Do

1 Flatten your bag on a table and use stickers and/or markers to make eyes, a nose, and a mouth on the flap part of the bag for the face of your doll.

2 To make the doll's hair, cut four strands of yarn. Put glue around the sides and top of the flap of the bag and press the yarn onto it.

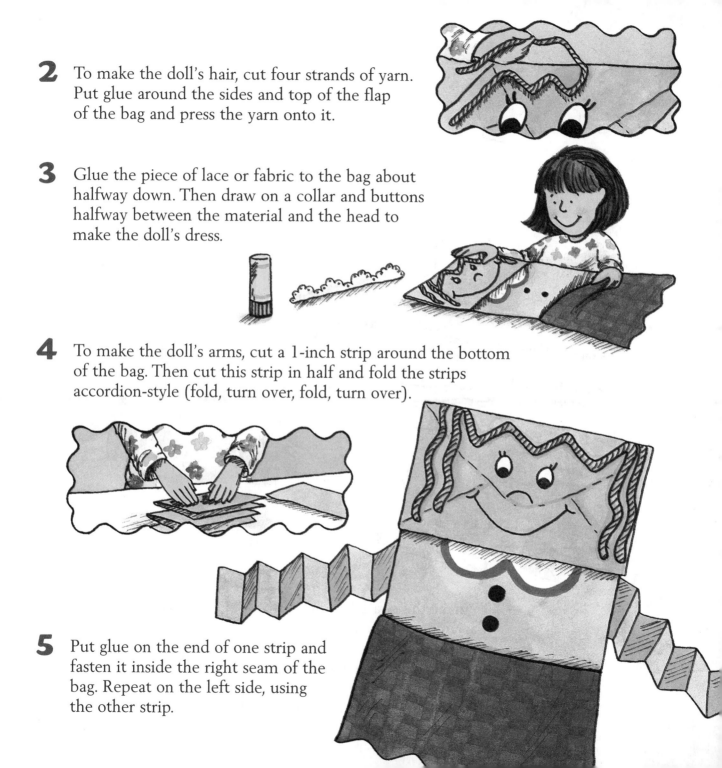

3 Glue the piece of lace or fabric to the bag about halfway down. Then draw on a collar and buttons halfway between the material and the head to make the doll's dress.

4 To make the doll's arms, cut a 1-inch strip around the bottom of the bag. Then cut this strip in half and fold the strips accordion-style (fold, turn over, fold, turn over).

5 Put glue on the end of one strip and fasten it inside the right seam of the bag. Repeat on the left side, using the other strip.

Giraffe Scissors Holder

This giraffe looks like a cute pet, but he's hiding a secret—your scissors!

What You Need

- 1 lunch-size brown paper bag
- 1 Styrofoam ball, about 2" in diameter
- safety scissors
- 1 rubber band or twist tie
- tape
- 1 sheet of construction paper (yellow or orange)
- crayons or non-toxic markers

What You Do

1 To make the giraffe's head, push a Styrofoam ball all the way down into the bag. Wrap the bag around the ball and close it with a rubber band or twist tie. Tape the open end of the bag closed.

2 Form the giraffe's neck by placing your hands under the balled head and twisting it a few times. The rest of the paper bag will be the giraffe's body.

3 Decorate the giraffe with crayons or markers, drawing his face and adding unique spots.

4 To make the giraffe's legs, cut four 2-inch x 6-inch rectangles from construction paper. Starting at the short end, roll one rectangle until you have a small log shape. Secure it with tape. Repeat with the other three rectangles.

5 Place the four rolls on the table so they are standing up and put a small loop of tape on the top of each one. Then take your giraffe body and position it over the four legs. Join them together by making sure the tape loops are secured to the bag.

6 Turning your new friend into a secret scissors holder is easy. Point your scissors down and push it into the Styrofoam ball. The circular finger-holds of your scissors will stick out the top, like little giraffe knobs.

Bonus Page

This page is a place for you to think up some of your own ideas for using paper bags. I'll start you off with one more.

Turn a large grocery-size bag into a cowboy vest!

1 Remove the bottom and slit the whole bag down the front.

2 Fringe it around the bottom by cutting the bag every inch or so.

3 Then cut an armhole in each side seam and decorate the bag with fun Western designs.

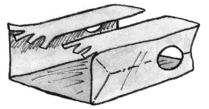